# BRITISH RAIL MOTIVE POWER IN THE 1980s

## ANDREW WALKER AND VAUGHAN HELLAM

AMBERLEY

First published 2023

Amberley Publishing
The Hill, Stroud
Gloucestershire, GL5 4EP

www.amberley-books.com

Copyright © Andrew Walker and Vaughan Hellam,
2023

The right of Andrew Walker and Vaughan Hellam
to be identified as the Author of this work has
been asserted in accordance with the Copyrights,
Designs and Patents Act 1988.

ISBN 978 1 3981 0922 3 (print)
ISBN 978 1 3981 0923 0 (ebook)

British Library Cataloguing in Publication Data.
A catalogue record for this book is available from
the British Library.

Origination by Amberley Publishing.
Printed in the UK.

# Introduction

The date is 31 December 1979. The location: Wakefield Kirkgate railway station. The authors of this book are standing in their duffel coats at the north end of the Up island platform, contemplating the approach of an unfitted goods train, hauled by a grubby Class 37 locomotive. It is a routine sight – just one of many such trains they will see that day, though unlike that particular one, most will be hauled by locomotives of types that can no longer be seen on the twenty-first century rail network. Tomorrow would mark the start of a new decade – the 1980s. To the young enthusiasts standing in the snow at Kirkgate, it sounds unfeasibly modern.

There is no doubt that on the last day of the 1970s, Britain's railways were in urgent need of modernisation, but while much of the infrastructure did date from pre-war times, the motive power was, in relative terms, quite new – most of the diesel and electric locomotives in service being only around fifteen to twenty years old. Despite this, the next decade would witness a dramatic contraction in numbers and in the variety of locomotive and multiple unit types, not simply because they became life-expired, though no doubt many did, but because of a transformation in the nature of the industries whose freight needs they served and in the demands and expectations of the travelling public who wanted faster, quieter and more modern trains. These changes saw the famous locomotive works at Derby, Crewe, Glasgow, Swindon and Doncaster become the equivalent of large-scale breakers' yards, cutting up virtually entire classes, while preservationists scrambled to accumulate sufficient funds to rescue the few individuals they could. To the credit of the dedicated enthusiasts who devoted their energies to this, many locomotives were saved, restored, and in some cases ultimately returned decades later to main line use, in a turnaround that simply could not be foreseen at that time.

It is true that the 1980s did see the construction of new motive power – for example the Class 58 – but this was on a scale that was far outweighed by the withdrawals. In an act of great irony, and one not only apparent in hindsight, the most modern rail tunnel in the country, the concrete-lined, illuminated, European gauge Woodhead New Tunnel, was rendered redundant when the route from Penistone to Hadfield was closed in 1981, a mere twenty-seven years after the bore had been completed. Soot-stained and crumbling Victorian-era tunnels elsewhere soldiered on.

In this book we have compiled a selection of pictures illustrating the diversity of BR's motive power in this decade of transformation. Our thanks go to fellow photographer John Walker for providing many of the images from his collection.

**Classic EE traction on Hellifield freight**
The 1980s dawned with the Class 40 fleet substantially intact and handling a wide range of freight and passenger duties. Here No. 40090 powers through Hellifield with bitumen tanks from the Stanlow refinery to Skipton in April 1980.

**A light engine manoeuvre for one of York's Deltics**
By now based at York rather than Haymarket, Deltic No. 55022 *Royal Scots Grey* is seen here running light engine towards the diesel depot at its new home in February 1980. The Deltic fleet was then down to twenty active members, but further withdrawals would soon follow.

**Classic Scottish Type 2 power**
For a good part of the decade, the smaller, medium-powered locomotives of Type 2 classification could find ample employment on passenger diagrams, particularly in Scotland. Here Class 27 No. 27050 departs Edinburgh Waverley with a northbound service in June 1985.

**Double-header at Manchester**
This pair of Type 2s looks to be more than sufficient for a relatively short freight working, seen here approaching Manchester Victoria in the summer of 1983. Two of the then still numerous Class 25s, Nos 25054 and 25080, are in charge. (J. M. Walker)

**From the capital to Norfolk by Brush Type 4**
In pre-electrification days, Class 47s powered most of the fast passenger services from London's Liverpool Street to East Anglia, achieving rapid timings over the relatively level terrain. Here No. 47569 waits to depart with a Norwich service in November 1981.

**Master of all trades**
Throughout the 1980s, the capable Class 47s were put to work on all manner of freight and passenger duties. Applying all of its Sulzer-powered output here, No. 47227 lifts a heavy aggregates train away from Peak Forest in the summer of 1988.

**Motive power diversity at Lincoln**
These bay platforms at the east end of Lincoln station served as a stabling point for locomotives between duties, and here we see regular pilot No. 08102 standing alongside Class 31 No. 31441 in 1987. The DMU fleet has not yet been completely displaced by Sprinters.

**A sign of things to come**
The disappearance of local freight yards and the decline in heavy industry that required shunting locomotives was not new to the 1980s, but the withdrawal of the several hundred strong Class 08 fleet moved up a gear in the early part of the decade. Here in 1983, several of the class are in the scrap lines at Swindon.

**The ubiquitous DMU**
A pair of BRCW diesel multiple units are
seen here at York in 1981. Away from the
third-rail electrified network of the South
East, units like these formed the backbone of
commuter services throughout the country.
Slam doors, sliding windows and a view
through the driver's cab were all features
that were to disappear with the advent of the
new Sprinter units.

**Signalling investment at Wakefield Kirkgate**
The signalling at Wakefield Kirkgate undergoes
modernisation in this 1982 view. All the
surviving semaphore signalling disappeared
at this time with the closure of the L&Y-era
signalbox. The station at Kirkgate, meanwhile,
was left in a disgracefully neglected state
throughout the decade and for many years
beyond. The two-car DMU on a Leeds service,
however, looks clean and smart.

**Engineering duty on the western region main line**
No. 31122 stands on the slow lines at Twyford on Sunday 15 April 1984 with an engineers' train. Most of these trains were composed of a selection of converted vehicles from an older generation. The second vehicle behind the brake van is a 'Salmon' wagon from LMS days with an added crane to hoist loads on and off the wagon.

**Class 31 on the old L&Y**
The former Lancashire & Yorkshire branch from Dewsbury East Junction to Dewsbury Market Place survives, albeit in truncated form, to handle freight traffic, latterly to a cement terminal. Here Class 31 No. 31174 runs light engine along the branch in August 1985.

**Scottish Type 2s receive attention at Derby**
A pair of Sulzer Class 27s stands among the visitors at Derby Works Open Day in 1982. A variant of the original Class 26, the 27s were a lighter and slightly more powerful machine and were fitted with GEC traction motors rather than the former's Crompton Parkinson units.

**Class 27 is centre of attention at Derby**
Looking somewhat like a candidate for scrapping at the works open day in September 1982, Sulzer Class 27 No. 27104 in fact emerged after repairs and was later renumbered as No. 27048. It lasted in traffic until 1986.

**Livery variations for West Coast electrics**
The 1980s saw the end of the era of all-over 'rail blue' as more eye-catching liveries began to appear. One such was the InterCity style, seen here carried by No. 87009 *City of Birmingham*, sharing the terminus at Manchester Piccadilly with No. 86238 in September 1984.

**Electric profiles at Piccadilly**
The angular form of a pair of Class 86s is seen in profile at Piccadilly in April 1982, both locomotives having worked in from Euston. Both 86/1 and 86/2 variants were rebuilds in 1972 from the original 'AL6' machines, with the 86/1s, of which only three existed, developing no less than 5,000 hp.

**Motive power profile at Toton**
A tidy line up at Toton in the form of Class 58 Nos 58027 and 58002, Class 20 Nos 20128, 20140 and 20124, and at the back, Class 56 No. 56008 – one of the original batch of Romanian-built machines first imported into the UK in 1976.

**Contrasting motive power in the paintshop**
By now many locomotives were paying their last visit to the Works, never to emerge, but in March 1984 there was still plenty of work for the paintshop at Crewe. Electric No. 86246 stands alongside Type 1 No. 20026, which is receiving a new coat of 'rail blue', a colour scheme in which it would see out its days on the BR network. (J. M. Walker)

**Departmental Gloucester R.C. & W. unit**
A number of diesel units found themselves in departmental use with BR when they were no longer required for passenger use. One is seen on an inspection trip here at Guide Bridge in 1982. Introduced in 1958, this Gloucester unit was equipped with two 6-cylinder 150-hp engines. Carrying the number TDB975227, it was formerly No. M55017.

**Parcels in transit at Victoria**
A small number of these Gloucester R.C. & W. Co. single 'motor parcels vans' were introduced in 1959. Here one of the rather functional-looking twin-engined units, No. M55990, is seen at Manchester Victoria East in the summer of 1980.

**A return to two-tone green**
Deltic D9000 *Royal Scots Grey* looks superb on display at Doncaster in 1986 following a repaint into its original livery of two-tone green, with the yellow frontal warning panel that was applied to most of the fleet by 1962. Delivered from Vulcan Foundry in February 1961, D9000 was first allocated to Haymarket.

**One of the fortunate few**
Deltic No. 55015 *Tulyar* has been taken out of the scrap line at Doncaster in February 1982 in readiness for its life in preservation. Many years of dedicated effort lie ahead for the enthusiasts who will restore and maintain this most complex of diesel locomotives. (J. M. Walker)

**A Deltic in its twilight days**
In their final months of operation, the Deltics found themselves operating on the Trans-Pennine route between York and Liverpool, once very unfamiliar territory. Here at Huddersfield, No. 55004 *Queens Own Highlander* has arrived with a westbound service in October 1981, with only days left before withdrawal.

**Deltic arrival at Doncaster**
In late 1981, enthusiasts were beginning to come to terms with the impending demise of the Deltics. By November, when this picture of No. 55008 *The Green Howards* was taken, the end was but weeks away. This will be one of its final journeys to London King's Cross.

**To South Wales in the sunshine**
There was plenty of locomotive-hauled mileage to be had in the early 1980s. In an era before multiple units took over most passenger services, Class 25 No. 25236 waits at Crewe with a service for Cardiff on a beautiful April afternoon in 1982.

**Class 31 chases rainbows at Barnsley**
A late summer shower has given way to bright sunshine at Barnsley on a Saturday morning in September 1980. Class 31 No. 31102 is at the northbound platform with a seasonal service for Llandudno, which it will work as far as Huddersfield.

**Heading for the hills**
A two-car DMU draws into a rather deserted-looking Hellifield station on 3 January 1986. At that time, as today, Hellifield was a stopping point on the Leeds to Morecambe service. The train will diverge from the Carlisle route at Settle Junction and take the Carnforth line to reach its coastal destination.

**Kirkby Stephen revival**
Closed in 1970, Kirkby Stephen lay unused until the restarting of local passenger services over the Settle & Carlisle in 1985. On 31 December 1986, a Carlisle to Skipton service prepares to stop at the station, which still displays the sign proclaiming 'Kirkby Stephen West', the name by which it was known at closure.

**The Permanent Way**
At Royston Junction in August 1980 there is a marked difference in the quality of track between the main line, where No. 40169 heads a train of ballast, and the freight lines beyond. The main line has welded rail and a speed limit of 50 mph, while the freight lines are maintained to a lower standard. Today only a single track remains here to serve the glass factory at Monk Bretton, near Barnsley.

**Lightweight load for split-headcode Type 4**
Heading two withdrawn Mk 1 carriages, No. 40131 passes Guide Bridge on 29 October 1982. To the left the engineers' sidings are busy, with a number of BR standard brake vans visible and one that dates from the days of the LMS.

**Penistone Goods**
One of the last Class 76s to be converted to air-brake-only, No. 76035 heads east past Penistone Goods with a short mixed freight on 18 June 1981. At this time, trains of mixed wagons were a feature of many routes.

**Woodhead wonder**
It's high summer at Penistone as vacuum-brake-only EM1 No. 76003 heads west on the Woodhead route after working a freight to Tinsley earlier in the day. It is 15 July 1980 and there is just over a year to go until closure. Remarkably, the photographer was the only person on the platforms that day.

**Vacuum only**
Type 1 Nos 20051 and 20069 are about to enter the Tunstead quarry complex at Great Rocks Junction with a rake of the famous ICI vacuum-brake hoppers on 6 August 1985. The last of these wagons were introduced in 1953 and would be in daily use until December 1997.

**Climbing round the curve at Oakenshaw**
A pair of Class 20s, with No. 20113 leading, grind around the steeply graded curve at Oakenshaw, near Wakefield, in May 1982. They will shortly gain the Midland main line and head south towards Sheffield.

**Options at Banbury**
Class 50 No. 50026 pauses at Banbury with a Birmingham New Street to Paddington service on 24 April 1984. If changing at Banbury, the traveller could opt to take the route to London Marylebone or a slow train for all stations to Oxford.

**Ready for the Works**
One of the features of the early 1980s was tatty corporate BR blue. Ready for a visit to Doncaster Works, where the Class 50 refurbishment programme was underway, No. 50024 *Vanguard* stands at Cheltenham with a train from Paddington on 21 April 1982.

**Classic backdrop for No. 55010**
Deltic No. 55010 *The King's Own Scottish Borderer* was deprived of one of its nameplates prior to withdrawal, for reasons unknown. Its anonymous side faces the camera here at York as it pauses beneath the magnificent roof with a Newcastle service in November 1981.

**Classic traction**
Locomotives were once the mainstay of passenger services through York. On 31 May 1982, 'Peak' No. 46037 had brought a special into York for the visit of Pope John Paul II. Many extra trains were laid on for the Pope's visit, all locomotive-hauled.

**The end is nigh**
A local DMU service to Dundee waits at Perth on 5 July 1988. With the introduction of Class 156 and 158 Sprinters, this BRCW unit would soon be sent to the breaker's yard.

**Cravens DMU on Leeds to Sheffield stopper**
Cravens unit Nos E51284 and E54558 stands at Barnsley on a snowy 8 January 1985. By today's standards the facilities here were basic, but at least there were staff, so passengers were updated on cancelled or late running trains. Many stations on the line were unstaffed halts with no communication systems whatsoever, so travellers would have no information if a train did not appear on time.

**Steam age reminders in rural Scotland**
Greenloaning, between Dunblane and Perth, harked back to the days of steam, with Up and Down goods loops to allow passenger trains to overtake slow moving freight. A local service for Perth heads north on 31 August 1988.

**Type 3 haulage on the Kyle line**
The Class 37s found useful employment right across the national network in the 1980s, and here at Achnasheen, No. 37260 *Radio Highland* is seen heading a Kyle of Lochalsh to Inverness service on a cool day in June 1985. Locomotive haulage on routes like this would soon give way to the 'Sprinter' units.

**Lincoln panorama**
There was still plenty of work available for Lincoln's regular station pilot, Class 08 No. 08102, when this picture was taken in 1987. One of its duties involved marshalling Royal Mail vans onto the daily TPO service to Crewe, which was invariably Class 31-hauled.

**Class 08 trip working**
Another image that illustrates the diversity of work carried out by the Class 08 fleet, as Healey Mills-based No. 08305 trundles towards the yard with a pair of tank wagons in the summer of 1986. The move probably originated at the nearby Procor wagon works.

**An unmistakeable landmark**
The distinctive outline of the tower dominates the skyline as a summer Saturday service pulls into the station at Blackpool North. For the haulage enthusiasts on board the train though, it is Class 40 No. 40009 that will be the centre of attention on this July afternoon in 1984. (J. M. Walker)

**A landscape soon to be transformed**
The passengers on board this Trans-Pennine service may not be aware that the view from their windows here at Wincobank, near Sheffield, will soon change out of all recognition. In the summer of 1984, Class 31 No. 31436 heads north past the site that will become the Meadowhall shopping centre. (J. M. Walker)

**Plenty going on at Hellifield**
In the early 1980s Hellifield was still an important location on the railway map. Sidings were used for storing ballast hoppers and recessing freights travelling over the Settle & Carlisle route, while crew changes took place on Anglo-Scottish freights. Here No. 31129 waits to work north with a train of hoppers while No. 40091 will move to the sidings on the other side of the station to take a ballast turn to Preston.

**Powering over the S&C**
A hazy August afternoon in 1984 sees a Leeds to Carlisle passenger service powering past Dent with Class 40 No. 40099 in charge, the driver giving a thumbs up to a pair of photographers hoping the line will be saved. The Midland-era signalbox was out of use at this time, and was demolished shortly after. The locomotive was cut up at Doncaster the following year.

**Steel goes west at Mirfield East**
After remodelling work took place in the early 1980s, the rationalised track layout between Ravensthorpe and Heaton Lodge Junction gave rise to Mirfield East Junction. Heading a steel train, No. 31324 accesses the goods loop on 21 April 1987.

**New order on the Hope Valley**
Refurbished ETH-fitted Class 31s were introduced on Trans-Pennine trains in the early 1980s, replacing the ageing Class 123 and 124 multiple units. On 1 October 1987, No. 31426 passes Edale with a train bound for Manchester Piccadilly.

**Vital cross-border grain traffic**
No. 40085 heads through Doncaster with a train of empty grain hoppers from the north-east of Scotland. The wagons would be destined for various parts of East Anglia, to be loaded with grain and taken back to Scottish distilleries for making whisky.

**Crewe-bound Class 40s at Guide Bridge**
This was a rather wet and grey day at Guide Bridge in April 1983, but Class 40 No. 40093 adds a splash of colour alongside classmate No. 40164 as they round the curve onto the Stockport lines en route from York MPD to Crewe Works for repairs. Unseen at the front, the motive power is being provided by Class 20 No. 20154.

**Norfolk DMU service**
A clean refurbished Metro-Cammell DMU passes the now closed Blue Circle cement terminal at Whitlingham Junction near Norwich in this image from the summer of 1986. The line to Cromer diverges to the left here, while the DMU is approaching on the route from Lowestoft and Yarmouth.

**High Wycombe reversal**
The line from Marylebone to High Wycombe was a veritable museum piece in the 1980s. Having arrived from London an eight-coach formation prepares to change direction at Wycombe and head a peak-hour service back to the capital in May 1984.

**Dependable performer at Garsdale**
'Generator' Class 47 No. 47418 approaches Garsdale with 1V90, a Glasgow Central to Penzance express, on 29 March 1986. One of the Brush Type 4 fleet that only carried two colour schemes throughout its working life – the blue seen here and the earlier two-tone green – it was also never named, unlike many of its Class 47/4 compatriots.

**Arten Gill memories**
The late 1980s saw a variety of liveries across the British Rail network. Here a mixture of BR blue and InterCity-liveried coaches, with 'large logo' No. 47440, crosses Arten Gill viaduct with a Leeds to Carlisle train on 4 March 1989.

**Coal for Lancashire on the Calder Valley route**
On the approaches to Healey Mills, No. 56018 heads a loaded MGR train, most likely bound for Fiddlers Ferry power station near Warrington, on 7 July 1983. Back in the 1980s, Healey Mills was still a busy location, with the shed having an allocation of locomotives.

**Powering the nation**
After the closure of Woodhead, all MGR traffic was diesel-hauled across the Pennines using Class 56s as motive power and taking a more circuitous route. Here in April 1983, No. 56026 brings MGR empties off the Stockport lines and through Guide Bridge before heading towards the Standedge route at Stalybridge.

**Crompton manoeuvre at St David's**
Exeter is blessed with two rail routes to London – one to Paddington and one to Waterloo. Having arrived at St David's on a service from London Waterloo, No. 33103 runs around its stock in preparation for the return journey on 10 August 1981. An array of classic lower quadrant semaphores can be seen behind.

**South Wales winter sunshine**
Bright December sunshine illuminates Type 3 No. 33027 at Cardiff Central in 1983. These locomotives were utilised extensively on the mid-Wales route to Crewe in the early years of the decade. (J. M. Walker)

**By AC electric to Euston**
In the early 1980s the principal passenger services from Glasgow, Liverpool and Manchester to London Euston were handled by the extensive fleet of AC electric locomotives of Classes 81 to 87. Here at Stockport in November 1981, Class 81 No. 81017 waits to depart with a service from Piccadilly.

**Class 83 in profile at Crewe**
First introduced in 1960, the English Electric Class 83 numbered only fifteen examples. Although visually almost identical to the other AC electrics in classes 81 to 85, it was the least powerful in terms of tractive effort. No. 83012 is seen here at Crewe in 1982. Withdrawn in 1983, it was later preserved.

**Easter diversion over the Blackburn-Hellifield line**
A bright spring day in 1989 sees Class 47 No. 47544 passing the closed station at Chatburn, during a weekend of diversions due to engineering work north of Preston. The passengers on this Glasgow–Penzance service will no doubt have enjoyed their spectacular journey over the Settle & Carlisle line.

**Another S&C diversion**
Brush Type 4 No. 47478 heads a Euston to Stranraer service off the Blackburn line and into Hellifield on 2 May 1987. From here, a pair of Class 31s was added to take the train north, giving those on board a rare triple-headed haulage experience.

**Type 1 light engine at Tinsley**
Type 1 No. 20228 leaves the reception sidings at Tinsley to join the rows of Class 20s on shed at the top left of the picture on 4 June 1982. The closure of Woodhead in July 1981 and withdrawal of the Class 76s saw the wires removed from the yard. At this date Tinsley had only a few more years to go before closure, but was still busy, with wagonload freight going strong. Today it is still a freight terminal but the marshalling yard is no more.

**Melancholy duty in the wake of closure**
Class 20 No. 20025 stands with a demolition train on the former Woodhead route at Shore Hall crossing near Penistone in December 1983. The protracted delay in track removal always meant there might be a chance of a reversal of the closure decision. Sadly, this was not to be and the remaining track was removed towards the end of 1986 on the eastern side of Woodhead tunnel.

**Piccadilly panorama**

This view of Manchester's Piccadilly terminus in September 1984 gives a good idea of the typical motive power to be seen here on a daily basis in those days. A service for Hull waits in platform 1 – the former Woodhead route departure point – with Class 31 No. 31444 in charge.

**Home territory for Crompton Type 3**

Class 33 No. 33106 is very much on home turf here at Clapham Junction. In September 1988, it is seen with a service from Waterloo, the passenger accommodation comprising '4TC' electric multiple unit stock. The Class 33/1s were modified to operate with these EMUs, thereby enabling access to non-electrified lines. (J. M. Walker)

**Conversation piece**
It is 22.55 on 3 September 1984 and the mailbags are lined up on the platform at Crewe waiting
to be loaded onto a northbound postal train. No. 87006 plays host to a conversation that no
doubt mentions the wet weather!

**Bringing the cheque and the postal order?**
Electric No. 85035 stands at Crewe while heading one of the many Travelling Post Offices that
passed through the station. Crewe was a major point at which trains connected and allowed
mail on the TPOs to be sorted, exchanged and sent on to the appropriate destination. Memories
still linger of the myriad of trains that once ran through this station at night, all now sadly gone.

**The centre of attention at Waverley**
Another Class 40-hauled railtour, the *St Andrew* ran from Bolton to Inverkeithing on 9 February 1985 and was plagued by train heating and timing problems throughout. Celebrity No. D200 provided the principal motive power, with classes 47 and 20 also putting in turns north of the border. (J. M. Walker)

**Taking a last look**
The Deltic fleet lasted a mere two years into the new decade. Here at Doncaster Works, crowds flocked to see the surviving machines courtesy of an open day organised by BREL on 27 February 1982. In this image, No. 55011 is flanked by Nos 55017 (left) and 55015 (right).

**Ravensthorpe Peak**
The layout at Ravensthorpe harked back to days when freight and passenger trains were separated by slow and fast lines. Heading towards Dewsbury, No. 45040 *King's Shropshire Light Infantry* approaches the station with a Liverpool to Newcastle train on 27 August 1983.

**Leaving Claydon on the former GCR**
Peak No. 45110 heads down the platform of the former Calvert station in Oxfordshire with a train of refuse containers returning from Claydon to Northolt. It is using the former 'Up' line of the Great Central route to Aylesbury, where it will then take the line to Princes Risborough and then continue its journey to London via High Wycombe.

**Seaside shunting duties**

The large coastal terminus of Scarborough is seen here in the summer of 1982. The many locomotive-hauled holiday season trains in those days required a station pilot to marshall the empty stock, and on this occasion No. 08540 is on duty. Locomotives were stabled in the yard on the right in between turns. (J. M. Walker)

**In the Swindon scrap line**

This rather forlorn sight was replicated at many of the BREL Works during the 1980s, as hundreds of locomotives met the cutter's torch. Here at Swindon in early 1983 is a rather skeletal No. 08505, alongside Nos 08553 and 25197. (J. M. Walker)

**A slight difference in aerodynamics**
Two locomotives that present rather contrasting cab designs are seen here at Birmingham New Street. In the days when a shunter still had reason to visit the station, No. 08740 stands alongside a Western Region HST set heading a cross-country service on April 1987.

**Semi-fast to Manchester**
A Class 304 EMU stands at Crewe in May 1980, prior to departure with an afternoon service for Manchester Piccadilly. These four-car units were built to a standard BR design in 1960 and were a familiar sight on the London Midland Region, operating out of London Euston and in the Birmingham, Manchester and Liverpool areas.

**Steam heating in order for Inverness passengers**
A steam-heated rake of locomotive hauled stock was still the order of the day for rail users in the mid-1980s. Here in 1985, Class 27 No. 27049 is warming up nicely at Inverness prior to departure for Thurso. The advent of the Sprinters would bring a dramatic change to many services like this one.

**'McRat' Rescue**
Having just brought in a failed Class 47, No. 26014 departs from Perth in August 1989. Locomotive haulage was still very much in evidence on services to Dundee, Aberdeen and Inverness. Change was coming in the shape of Class 158 Express Sprinters, which would dominate services from the early 1990s.

**Dunford West MGR**
Several Class 76s were converted to air brake only for MGR trains over Woodhead during the 1970s. Two of this series, Nos 76032 and 76034, head a train of empty MGR hoppers back to Yorkshire on 15 July 1981, just two days before the last train of coal would pass through Woodhead tunnel.

**The way freight used to be**
In the 1980s 'loose-coupled' freights were phased out in favour of vacuum- or air-braked loads. Subsequently, air braking would survive and vacuum brakes would be consigned to history. Heading a loose-coupled set of mineral wagons with brake van at the rear, No. 76028, with both vacuum and air brake capability, heads through Dunford West towards the eastern portal of Woodhead tunnel.

**Steady progress for Immingham-bound freight**
Class 37 No. 37203 creeps around the back of the station at Brocklesby on 24 July 1987 with a mixed load of air-braked wagons destined for Immingham. Although fitted with vacuum brakes when built, air brakes became standard and No. 37203 was additionally fitted with these in the early 1970s.

**HST navigates coal-mining territory**
A southbound HST set working a NE–SW service negotiates the crossover from the former goods to main line at Royston Junction in May 1982. The two main line tracks on the right are out of use due to subsidence, a persistent blight for the railway in this area of Yorkshire.

**Classic Type 4 traction in Ribblesdale**
The Settle & Carlisle line had not long been reprieved from the threat of closure when this picture was taken in the summer of 1985. Although train services were rather infrequent on the passenger timetable, there was the consolation of haulage behind celebrity Type 4 No. 40122, seen here at Horton-in-Ribblesdale.

**Sought-after traction for 1980s railtours**
As the 1980s progressed, Class 40s found themselves in demand for enthusiast railtours. Knowing that the class would not see the decade out, operators organised tours with the classic Type 4 traction, as seen here at Montrose in March 1984 with No. 40086 receiving much interest from photographers.

**Morning Freightliner**
Brush Type 4 No. 47330 powers through Cudworth with a Southampton to Leeds freightliner
on 12 July 1983. The former station here closed on 1 January 1968, at a time when it was
thought that roads would carry the passengers of the future and the railways would move freight
instead. The platform edges at Cudworth were removed, which allowed the track to be realigned
for trains to pass through at greater speed.

**Sheffield landscape set to change**
With Tinsley Viaduct dominating the background, No. 47600 heads towards Wincobank
Junction and is passing what is now the station at Meadowhall, on 7 August 1984. During the
1980s many Class 47s were undergoing works overhauls, being outshopped from Crewe with
electric train heating as standard.

**Cross-country expedition**
Diverted off the WCML due to engineering work, No. 47527 heads the 08.12 Manchester
to Glasgow and Edinburgh over the little used Clitheroe to Hellifield line near Rimington.
Consistent with the time, the train comprises a variety of types of BR coaching stock ranging
from Mk 1 to different generations of Mk 2 vehicles.

**Busy Hellifield**
Hellifield was a popular spot to photograph the locomotive-hauled passenger services that were
frequently diverted over the Settle & Carlisle line in the 1980s due to engineering works on the
West Coast. Here No. 47509 *Albion* approaches going south while a triple-headed service heads
north, with a pair of Class 31s helping an apparently ailing No. 47478.

**Steam heat was all part of the experience**
An early morning on a summer Saturday in 1981, and Class 31 No. 31235 clearly has the steam heating in full working order as it pulls into Barnsley station with the seasonal Llandudno service. It's June, but no doubt the passengers will appreciate the additional warmth courtesy of their Type 2 motive power.

**Newspapers from seaside to city**
The Cleethorpes to Manchester newspapers and parcels train was a regular Class 40 working until the final withdrawal of the fleet on 22 January 1985. With just a few weeks to go in regular service, No. 40086 waits at Sheffield Midland having arrived from Cleethorpes on 9 January 1985. On the left No. 31298 waits with a short engineers' train.

**Ready to go**

The Class 81s were introduced in 1959 for the electrification of the West Coast route out of Euston. Here No. 81008 sits in the loco holding sidings at Wolverhampton ready to take over a cross-country service in the spring of 1986. The white salmon logo on the side was a sign the loco was allocated to Motherwell depot.

**Unique electric prototype**

Built as a prototype electric locomotive in 1986, unique Brush No. 89001 is seen at Doncaster on 9 September 1989. Built at Derby's Litchurch Lane works, it was named *Avocet* by Prime Minister Margaret Thatcher in January 1989. No. 89001 worked passenger services prior to the Class 91s being introduced on the ECML.

**Special purpose vehicles**
The eighties was a time when some rather unusual workings could still run with unique rolling stock. Heading a train of UKF phosphoric acid tanks, No. 56111 passes Mirfield in August 1984. These tanks were usually found working between Ince and Corkicle, so it is assumed that this was a special working.

**Privately-owned pioneer on the Berks & Hants route**
Foster Yeoman No. 59002 passes the lock at Froxfield with an empty train of 'Jumbo' aggregate wagons on 21 June 1986. At this time, the Class 59s were the only private locomotives working on British Rail, though they were manned by BR drivers. They demonstrated the ability to haul 4,500-ton trains and in the late 1990s would pave the way for the Class 66s.

**Survivor of the steam-age timetable**
In the 1980s timetable there were remnants of loco-hauled trains from a previous age, which in modern times have been reinstated. Whereas most trains on the Chiltern lines ran between Marylebone and Banbury, where passengers for Birmingham would have to change, one evening train ran instead from Paddington direct to Birmingham. Here No. 50039 leaves High Wycombe on 29 March 1984, bound for New Street.

**An ex-works Type 4 on the Chilterns route**
The line from Banbury was dominated by DMUs in the 1980s, apart from a morning and evening working to and from Paddington also serving the West Midlands, which was loco-hauled. The evening train could be pot luck in terms of rolling stock and traction – on this occasion in 1984, ex-works No. 50038 heads up Saunderton rise with a uniform Mk 1 rake.

**All consigned to history**
The large brick-built motive power depot at Reddish, constructed to coincide with the electrification of the Woodhead route, has long since been demolished and the site cleared. In better times, Class 25 No. 25326 and Type 4 No. 40141 rest outside the shed on a summer's evening in July 1982.

**A Scottish visitor at Crewe**
One of the early Sulzer Type 2 designs, the Class 26s were always associated with Scotland, but here in May 1980 No. 26013 is unusually seen awaiting attention at Crewe works. Forty-seven examples were built from 1958 prior to the introduction of the slightly more powerful Class 27 variant.

**Reversal of fortunes for Wath coal traffic**
Closure of the Woodhead route in July 1981 and then the removal of track from the western end of Wath Yard at Elsecar Junction left remaining coal traffic from Manvers Main having to reverse at Wath Central. On 8 September 1986, No. 56072 runs around a loaded MGR train before taking the line towards Doncaster.

**Rails salvaged, but railway history lost**
Closure of the Woodhead route in July 1981 left a bitter taste for many in the rail industry. While the Wath branch was rapidly dismantled between Wombwell Main and West Silkstone Junction, the line from Deepcar to Hadfield remained for five years. Demolition ultimately came though, as witnessed here with No. 47371 about to access the closed railway at Penistone on 5 January 1987 with a salvage train.

**DMU alongside an ancient highway**
Class 119 DMU set No. L572 passes the lock at Froxfield on the Kennet & Avon Canal. It is working a local service down the Berks & Hants route towards Bedwyn on 21 June 1986. The Class 119s were built as cross-country units, similar in layout to the Swindon Class 120 units, by the Gloucester Railway Carriage & Wagon Company. They were a very successful design and lasted until the mid-1990s before final withdrawal.

**Crowds gather to say farewell**
The date is January 1983, and this is the station at Clayton West on the last day of passenger services. A BRCW unit stands in the platform having arrived with a fully loaded service from Huddersfield. The 4-mile branch from Shepley was first opened by the L&Y in 1879. (J. M. Walker)

**Locomotive haulage over the beautiful S&C**
Passengers on the Settle & Carlisle line in the 1980s had a limited choice of trains, but nearly all were locomotive hauled, with Classes 31, 40, 45 and 47 making regular appearances. Here No. 31404 goes north at Dent with a short rake of Mk 1 coaches in April 1983.

**Autumn at Earles Sidings**
The Class 31s were given a new lease of life following their refurbishment at Doncaster Works and subsequent allocation to the Trans-Pennine services via the Hope Valley to replace Class 123 and 124 DMUs. Here No. 31437 heads for Sheffield at Earles Sidings in October 1987.

**Great British landscape**
On a typically cloudy August day in 1985, No. 47508 *Great Britain* heads north at Arten Gill with a Leeds to Carlisle train. The eleven-arch viaduct here is 117 feet high and constructed of what is known as Dent marble.

**Diverted through the Lancashire hills**
During the 1980s, diversions from the WCML north of Preston by way of the Settle and Carlisle were commonplace in late winter and early spring. This brought much activity to the normally little-used line between Hellifield and Clitheroe. Here No. 47441 heads north near Rimington with the 07.25 Birmingham to Edinburgh on 11 March 1989.

**Farewell to the Deltics**
Deltic No. 55007 *Pinza* stands at Doncaster Works on the occasion of the farewell event in
February 1982. Fifteen of the survivors were gathered together to allow enthusiasts a last chance
to see and photograph these legendary machines before the majority were despatched to the
scrapyard. (J. M. Walker)

**Living on borrowed time**
Seen here in 1983, Class 42 'Warship' No. D818 *Glory* was a static exhibit outside BREL's
Swindon Works for several years following its withdrawal in 1972. Officially a 'Departmental'
machine, a decision was made to scrap the loco on site in 1985, thereby depriving the preservation
movement an opportunity to restore one of the few remaining diesel-hydraulics. (J. M. Walker)

**Light engine beneath the lower quadrants**
Class 56 No. 56112 was less than a year old when this shot was taken in December 1982.
Passing semaphore signals that are considerably older, the Doncaster-built machine is somewhat
unusually seen running light engine through High Wycombe, possibly on a crew training run.

**The new generation on merry-go-round duty**
Doncaster-built Type 5 No. 58018 *High Marnham Power Station* approaches Attenborough,
near Nottingham, with a rake of MGR hoppers in July 1988. The locomotive was built in the
summer of 1984 and is only four years old in this picture.

**A machine of many identities**
One of the longest serving Class 86s, No. 86412 stands at Birmingham New Street in 1987.
A series of renumberings to reflect changes to mechanical specification saw the original
No. 86012 subsequently carry numbers 86312, 86412 and finally 86612, in which guise it still
operates more than fifty years after its introduction in 1965.

**New arrivals for the East Coast Main Line**
A batch of Driving Van Trailers destined for the new Class 91-hauled ECML services is seen
here at Preston in June 1989. Class 86 No. 86425 was later repainted into the red livery of Rail
Express Systems and named *Saint Mungo*. It was scrapped at Booth's of Rotherham in 2004.

**Hanger on**
While many Scottish internal services would soon be in the hands of Class 158s, the Inverness to Euston service was Class 47-hauled into the early 1990s. About to depart from Perth in the summer of 1989, No. 47633 will give way to electric traction at Mossend 'yard' before the train heads south over the border.

**Class 47 at a busy south-western hub**
Exeter St David's was a station with plenty of interest in the locomotive-hauled years of the early 1980s. Class 33s from the Southern Region frequently mixed with other locomotives such as Classes 45, 46, 47 and 50 all regularly passing through. Here No. 47554 heads a service from Paddington on 10 August 1981.

**Trans-Pennine coal duties**
At the time of this picture, recently built Class 56 No. 56093 was based at Healey Mills depot, and was a regular performer on Trans-Pennine MGR duties. Here it is seen at Huddersfield with a returning rake of empties from Lancashire in November 1981.

**Before the vegetation took over**
Class 56 No. 56110 waits to leave Healey Mills yard with an empty MGR service in the summer of 1985. This locomotive later found itself rusting away among the many condemned Class 56s languishing in the yard following withdrawal. Years of contraction and neglect later led to the yard itself being largely overgrown with trees and shrubs.

**Banbury Brush**
Passing Banbury on 4 April 1984, No. 47306 heads what is a short train of containers by today's standards. There were still two signal boxes here in the 1980s, Banbury North and Banbury South. Inter-regional freights would still swap locomotives here too, usually being lined up just to the right-hand side of this picture.

**Decline of local power generation**
A feeling of dereliction has crept into Ravensthorpe as the sidings that once fed the power station off to the left have been removed and most trains will pass through on their way to somewhere else. No. 47509 *Albion* approaches the station with a westbound Trans-Pennine express in August 1983.

**Piccadilly panorama in the era of rail blue**
This panoramic view of Manchester's Piccadilly terminus in 1984 shows to good effect the monopoly of 'rail blue' livery in those days. Amid a haze of exhaust fumes, which are also a thing of the past, numerous multiple units – both diesel and electric – await departure on a multitude of local and cross-country services.

**Skipton memories**
A Sunday in December 1986, and Skipton appears hardly changed since the days of steam, retaining artefacts such as water columns, signal boxes and old Midland Railway wooden signal posts. The traction had changed though, with DMUs taking over local services and diesel locomotives on trains to quarries on the Grassington branch. Here a Class 31 and a couple of DMUs wait to work Monday morning trains.

**Overnight parcels turn for Sulzer Type 2**
The Class 25s were put to work on a variety of duties and this was a typical turn for No. 25229. The rather work-stained machine is seen at Crewe with one of the many overnight parcels and newspaper trains that routinely called here in the days when this traffic was largely carried by rail.

**Sulzer Type 2 on shed**
Smart-looking Class 25 No. 25044 stands outside the shed at Edinburgh's Haymarket depot in September 1980. This particular Type 2, a Class 25/1 variant, was steam-heat fitted and dual-braked, making it a particularly versatile machine. At this time there were around 300 Class 25s in service. (J. M. Walker)

**No. 03066 at Newcastle**
The characterful Gardner-engined Class 03s numbered over 120 examples in 1973, but by 1985 when this photograph was taken, they had dwindled to just a handful in service. Retained as a station pilot, this is No. 03066 puffing away gently in Newcastle's Central station on a chilly February morning. (J. M. Walker)

**A change of livery for No. 08499**
While many Class 08s were withdrawn and scrapped in the 1980s, for those that survived and were still required for shunting duties, there was sometimes a well-deserved refurbishment on the cards. One recipient of a smart new two-tone grey colour scheme was No. 08499, seen here at Toton TMD in August 1988.

**A celebration of Scottish identity at Dundee**
DMU No. 101319 was branded with a 'Bathgate Link' logo in 1984 to mark the reopening of the station at Bathgate and inauguration of the service to Edinburgh. During the 1980s, BR departed from its corporate image to celebrate local and regional identity, one of the most famous being 'Scotrail', introduced in 1985 and still used today. Here the unit waits at Dundee in July 1988 with a service to Arbroath.

**Cleethorpes bound**
A refurbished two-car Metro-Cammell DMU is seen here approaching Brocklesby Junction station in April 1987. At this time the new generation Pacer units were already in service but the long-serving DMU fleet still had some years left. Brocklesby itself was closed to passengers in 1993.

**A long-gone Yorkshire junction**
Goosehill Junction was where the line for Wakefield Kirkgate and Healey Mills diverged from the Midland main line to Sheffield via Royston Junction and Cudworth. On 11 July 1983, not very much has changed since the days of steam as No. 47121 passes with an engineer's train featuring an ex-GWR brake van besides the usual BR standard type.

**Summer at Cudworth**
A visitor to Cudworth today would find only the remains of a railway and might never guess that they were looking at a former four-track main line that carried express passenger services and freight. In June 1981, Cudworth boasted semaphore signals and three signal boxes within a short distance of each other. Here Nos 20005 and 20096 head a train of scrap metal towards Sheffield.

**Not just passenger traffic at Sheffield**
The days of parcels and mail being transported by rail are evoked by the mail bag and the
'BRUTE' trolley on platform 7 at Sheffield. Almost incidental to the scene, Peak No. 45111 ends
its journey from St Pancras and will soon run around its train to return south on 10 May 1983.

**A Peak on familiar tracks**
The Standedge route from Leeds to Huddersfield saw regular locomotive-hauled trains serving
Liverpool, Newcastle and Scarborough during the 1980s. On 13 July 1983, Peak No. 45136
heads a train east through Marsden.

**Type 2s out, Type 3s in for Scottish services**
Locomotive haulage was a common feature of Scottish trains in the 1980s. It would largely come to an end with the introduction of the Class 158 Sprinters in 1990. In the mid-1980s, the Scottish Type 2s were replaced with newly converted Class 37/4s with electric train heating. Awaiting its next turn, No. 37408 sits at the buffers at Glasgow Queen Street on 27 March 1987.

**Highland 37s wait to go at Fort William**
Back in the 1980s services to and from the highland terminus of Fort William were exclusively Class 37-hauled. On 28 March 1987, No. 37425 waits to depart with a Mallaig train whilst on the left, No. 37406 is ready to depart with a train to Glasgow Queen Street.

**Limestone through the Peak**
The heavy limestone trains leaving Tunstead quarry during the early 1980s were entrusted to Class 25 locomotives. Such trains required banking assistance from Great Rocks Junction to Peak Forest, before the banker would drop off and the train would continue with a sole Type 2. On 25 September 1981, No. 25081 takes a train of ICI bogie hoppers through the much-diminished Chinley station.

**Reversal at Claydon**
The Calvert Waste Disposal facility was on the former Great Central railway line between Aylesbury and Claydon Junction, near Bicester. Waste from Northolt transfer station in London was sent here to fill the former clay quarries. Having arrived with a train of loaded containers, No. 45110 reverses the return train of empties onto the former Great Central Up line.

**In the days of the marshalling yards**
Healey Mills, seen here in 1986, was one of many large marshalling yards constructed mainly in the 1960s to improve the efficiency of regional freight handling. As the need to combine and separate wagonloads declined in the 1980s though, these yards lost their importance and those that survive now are a shadow of their former selves.

**Diggle diversion**
After a train of fuel tankers caught fire in Summit tunnel in December 1984, closing the Calder Valley line, freight traffic was diverted via the Diggle route. On 19 August 1985 No. 56075 heads a diverted train of MGR empties approaching Diggle Junction, just prior to the reopening of the tunnel.

**Not quite the end for an AC electric**
This is Crewe in March 1984, with Class 85 No. 85033 being stripped for spares. The locomotive was briefly reunited with its bogies but never left the confines of the works, being cut up there in 1985 after a twenty-five-year working life. (J. M. Walker)

**Southern Region workhorse for the commuter belt**
One of the Southern Region's characteristic EMUs, 4-VEP unit No. 7837 stands at Farnham on 28 March 1983. Built at York from 1967 to 1974, these units were the last to feature manually opening doors next to every seating row.

**A real gathering of motive power**
Scenes like this have largely disappeared from the national network, with one or two exceptions. In 1983, however, it was commonplace to see large numbers of locomotives stabled at the many depots around the country. This is Crewe, with both diesel and electric motive power in attendance. (J. M. Walker)

**A sea of blue**
It was common to see large numbers of rail blue-liveried locomotives gathered at the numerous motive power depots around the country in the 1980s. Although alternative liveries had started to appear early in the decade, here at Cardiff Canton in 1983 the uniform of the corporate fleet prevails. (J. M. Walker)

**Brush Type 2 on shed at Colchester**
There was no main line diesel allocation at Colchester in the early 1980s, but the shed, located immediately opposite the passenger station platforms, was host to numerous locomotives that were stabling between turns. Here No. 31138 stands in the sunshine in May 1982.

**Toton transition**
Toton depot in the summer of 1988 sees Class 56 No. 56075 sharing the yard with Class 37 No. 37374, which was formerly No. 37165, and which subsequently reverted to the latter identification. By now the familiar 'Peaks' and Class 25s once associated with this depot had all but gone, with only a couple of withdrawn examples still to be found here.

**Class 85 in winter sunshine**
This is the view looking north at Carlisle on a bright November day in 1984. Class 85 No. 85039 is approaching the station with a southbound parcels service. Forty of these 3,200-hp machines were built for the West Coast electrification in 1960. Withdrawals began in the mid-1980s, though some lasted into the early 1990s. (J. M. Walker)

**APT – the vision that was not to be**
The innovative tilting Advanced Passenger Train was to prove unsuccessful in commercial service and only six trains were ever built, each comprising six articulated coaches, with a single central power car. The trains generally operated in pairs to provide a twelve-coach formation. No. 370002 departs Crewe in August 1984. (J. M. Walker)

**Stranraer-bound**

Adorned in Network SouthEast livery, No. 47582 is a long way from home at Glasgow Central on a Stranraer-bound train on 9 October 1987. Over the years Stranraer has sadly lost its importance on the rail network. Served today primarily by a rather sparse service to Kilmarnock, at one time it could boast direct passenger trains to and from Euston.

**Varied history of the D400 class**

Introduced on the West Coast main line between Crewe and Glasgow before electrification, the Class 50s became the only 100-mph diesel locomotive after withdrawal of the Deltics in 1982. When electrics took over West Coast services in 1974, the Class 50s moved to the Western Region to replace the diesel-hydraulics. In turn the InterCity 125 HSTs ousted the Class 50s during the 1980s. Here No. 50009 waits at Paddington in April 1984 with a train for Reading and Oxford.

**AC electric variety at Piccadilly, 1984**
Class 86 No. 86238 waits to depart Manchester Piccadilly on a London service while a Class 304 EMU stands in the through platforms. The EMU has undergone a refurbishment and looks smart in its new InterCity blue and grey colour scheme. Forty-five of these units were introduced in 1960–62 and were withdrawn in the mid-1990s.

**Double-headed electrics at Carlisle**
First introduced in 1959, the Class 81 was built for BR by AEI, and was a powerful machine developing over 3,000 hp. Here at Carlisle we see Nos 81002 and 81007 getting to grips with a loaded aggregates train on a rainy August day in 1987. (J. M. Walker)

**One of the great survivors**
The three-car GEC-powered Class 506 electric multiple units were introduced on the Manchester–Hadfield–Glossop route in 1954, and were designed to operate with the 1,500V DC current that served the Woodhead electrification. Here at Piccadilly in 1984, unit No. 59403 is in its twilight years.

**Sprinters herald the new era on Scottish services**
The late 1980s saw the replacement of locomotive-hauled trains on ScotRail services with Class 156 and Class 158 Sprinters. On 26 August 1989, two 156s, one from Fort William and one from Oban, have joined at Crianlarich to form a Glasgow train. On the right, representing the 'old school', No. 37401 waits to depart for Fort William.

**A grim evening at Crewe**
There's no cover available for this Class 08 as it awaits its next turn of duty on a soaking wet
September night in 1984. Crewe was a major hub for overnight parcels traffic in the 1980s, and
no doubt No. 08927 would be kept busy through the early hours.

**A new lease of life**
Many shunting locomotives found a new purpose in life following their withdrawal from the
national network. Here at Peak Forest Sidings in the summer of 1983, one of the Ruston &
Hornsby-built Class 07s, No. 07001, has been put to good use marshalling the many aggregate
trains that originate at the nearby quarries. (J. M. Walker)

**Echoes of the past at Shrub Hill**
Heading a train of vacuum-braked four-wheelers, No. 31149 heads into Worcester Shrub Hill
on 16 August 1985. Very few bogie freight wagons existed in the 1980s and many vehicles were
survivors from the steam age. The gradual introduction of air-braked bogie wagons spelled the
end for non-fitted freight trains by the end of the decade.

**Cromptons double up on containers**
The most powerful of the Bo-Bo diesel types of the day, the Class 33s were found predominantly
in the south and west of the country. They were not commonly seen in pairs, but here Nos 33032
and 33017 are teamed to work a container service at Waltham St Lawrence on the west of
England main line in June 1984.

**Sulzer Type 2 on home territory**
Edinburgh's Haymarket depot was home to a large allocation of motive power in the 1980s, including a number of Class 27s. Here in November 1981, No. 27023 stands outside the shed with a Class 26 behind. Like many traction maintenance depots, Haymarket eventually became a servicing point primarily for multiple units.

**Motive power variety at Toton**
Visiting a motive power depot with a 'permit' was all part of the 1980s routine, and a typical weekend at a major depot like Toton provided the opportunity to capture large numbers of locos 'on shed'. By 1988, Class 58s were well established here, and a few Class 20s were clinging on.

**Classic Type 4 territory**
Having sustained minor accident damage, thankfully not enough for write-off, No. 40131 stands at Guide Bridge waiting to enter the stabling point on 29 October 1982. At the time, Guide Bridge and the surrounding area became a Mecca for Class 40 enthusiasts.

**Class 40 portion**
The 1980s saw some passenger trains timetabled to combine and split en route. Class 40 No. 40012, formerly *Aureol*, stands at York with the Sheffield to Newcastle portion of a train from Poole.

**The way it used to be**
A permit to visit the works at Crewe was always an eagerly anticipated event for the young
enthusiast. This is a typical scene in 1984 as a group of lads surveys Class 20 No. 20065, one of
several Type 1s receiving attention in the repair shops. (J. M. Walker)

**Awaiting its final repaint**
A last sighting of veteran Type 1 No. 20023 in standard BR rail blue, at Derby Works in March
1985. It would emerge in new 'large logo' grey livery with full yellow cabs and red solebar, in
which livery it would see out its final years on the network. It was scrapped at MC Metals in
Glasgow in 1992. (J. M. Walker)

**Type 1 pairing at Kirkgate**
The single-cab Class 20 was a particularly versatile machine when operated in a pair, and this
was by far the most common configuration. One of the notable successes of BR's Modernisation
Plan, over 200 examples were built. Here Nos 20011 and 20154 run light engine through
Wakefield Kirkgate in 1980.

**Twilight years of a once extensive network**
After Woodhead was abandoned, the infrastructure that fed into the route began to be closed.
The yard at Wath was built to handle coal traffic from many surrounding collieries, which BR
said was declining. On 31 March 1983, No. 31151 stands with an engineers train on the main
line at Wath while Nos 20154 and 20054 occupy the remains of the yard.

**Always a special case**
Forty-eight Class 73 electro-diesels were built by BR and English Electric between 1962 and 1965. Devoted to the Southern Region for most of their working lives, these unusual locomotives could operate from the third rail electrification, or with their 600-hp diesel engine. In September 1988, No. 73201 *Broadlands* approaches Clapham Junction. (J. M. Walker)

**Suitably Scottish**
The only Class 47/4 to carry the 'blue stripe' version of InterCity livery, No. 47461 *Charles Rennie Mackintosh* pulls into Perth in lieu of a 47/7 variant on an Aberdeen service in the summer of 1989. Sadly it was only to last another year in traffic, being withdrawn after a shunting mishap at Liverpool.

**A Deltic in winter**

On a chilly 2 February 1980, No. 55004 *Queens Own Highlander* leaves Doncaster with a northbound express. Whatever the weather, a Deltic was to be revered, especially when it had just less than two years left in BR service.

**Refurbishment at Doncaster**

Class 50 No. 50036 *Victorious* makes a superb sight at the Doncaster Works open day in May 1986. Previously refurbished at Doncaster when it would have first received 'large logo' livery, this would be its final repaint, as it was to be condemned in 1991 and cut up at nearby Booth's scrapyard in Rotherham the following year.

**Aureol arrives at Doncaster**
A sunny Saturday morning at Doncaster in May 1982, and Class 40 No. 40012 *Aureol* pulls into platform 4 with a Manchester service, the leading coaches full of the many enthusiasts for whom haulage on these trains in the early 1980s was a mandatory weekend experience. (J. M. Walker)

**All quiet at Manchester Victoria**
A classic location for diesel photography in the 1980s, Victoria has been transformed in recent years and now bears little resemblance to the scene we see here in 1980. One of the 'split headcode' cohort of Class 40s, No. 40136 stands at a remarkably quiet platform with an inspection saloon.

**Before the Type 2 takeover**
Class 124 Trans-Pennine units began working services via Sheffield in 1977 along with the Class 123 'Swindon' units. In a rare turn of events, the Class 124s would be ousted by locomotive-hauled stock using Class 31s in 1984. On 25 September 1981, a train from Manchester slows for Chinley North Junction to take the Hope Valley line.

**Passing Hellifield**
A Morecambe to Leeds semi-fast passes Hellifield in April 1983. The train is formed of a four-car Swindon-built InterCity unit transferred from the Western Region in the late 1970s to provide increased capacity on Trans-Pennine routes. When built in 1961 these units had route indicator panels beneath the cab windows.

**Class 20s in attendance for Crewe engineering work**
Track relaying and associated resignalling work at Crewe took place in the mid-1980s, and here in September 1984, Class 20s Nos 20166 and 20151 are in attendance on a rain-soaked night.

**Making room on shed**
Class 20 No. 20031 heads a line of locomotives being shunted off the depot at York to provide room for stabling of incoming locomotives on the numerous additional trains on the occasion of the Pope's visit in May 1982. Also in this line-up are Nos 25044, 31283, 31280 and 37192. (J. M. Walker)

**Overnight activity at Crewe**
In the 1980s, Crewe was busy throughout the night. The early hours of 11 April 1985 see Class 86 No. 86248 *Sir Clwyd/County of Clwyd* awaiting departure with the southbound *Irish Mail*. On the right, No. 86103 *Andre Chapelon* waits with another London-bound working.

**AC electric contrasts at Carlisle**
Class 81 electric No. 81013, on a train of empty sleeper stock, stands alongside a relative newcomer in the form of Class 86 No. 86329, built a few years later. The Class 86 was the most numerous of the AC 'West Coast' electrics, numbering a hundred examples. This picture was taken in November 1984. (J. M. Walker)

**Deltic Farewell tour arrives at Waverley**
Deltic No. 55009 *Alycidon* has just arrived at Edinburgh's Waverley station with one of BR's official 'farewell' tours on 28 November 1981. The circular trip took passengers from Newcastle to the Scottish capital via Carlisle, and then back via the East Coast Main Line.

**Alycidon takes a break at Haymarket**
Deltic No. 55009 *Alycidon* was in sparkling condition for this official BR 'farewell' tour in
November 1981. Having run light engine from Waverley station, No. 55009 rests at Haymarket
depot prior to the return leg to Tyneside.

**Not long to go for Woodhead**
Not many more MGR trains will follow Nos 76032 and 76034 heading westbound out of Woodhead tunnel on 14 July 1981. The last MGR train would leave Barnsley Junction sidings on the evening of 18 July, ending the transport of Yorkshire coal via Woodhead.

**Into the tunnel and into history**
Yorkshire coal contributed to power generation in the 1980s with flows to Fiddlers Ferry, near Warrington, being part of the mix. Nos 76010 and 76016 head a train of empties and are about to pass the tiny redundant platforms at Woodhead on 14 July 1981. The line was closed just four days later; the week after, coal would be diesel-hauled across the Pennines via the Standedge route.

| | | |
|---|---|---|
| Class 50 | 50 | 38 |
| Class 55 | 20 | 0 |
| Class 56 | 71* | 135 |
| Class 58 | N/A | 50 |
| Class 59 | N/A | 5 |
| **Total** | **3,444** | **2,010** |

Source: *British Rail Motive Power Combined Volume 1980*, Ian Allan Ltd (1979); *British Rail Locomotives 1990*, Ian Allan Ltd (1990)

Except *: authors' own data

## Electric Locomotives

| | **At 31 December 1979** | **At 31 December 1989** |
|---|---|---|
| Class 73 | 48 | 47 |
| Class 76 | 40 | 0 |
| Class 81 | 22 | 5 |
| Class 82 | 8 | 0 |
| Class 83 | 14 | 0 |
| Class 84 | 4 | 0 |
| Class 85 | 40 | 25 |
| Class 86 | 100 | 99 |
| Class 87 | 36 | 36 |
| Class 89 | N/A | 1 |
| Class 90 | N/A | 50 |
| Class 91 | N/A | 35 |
| **Total** | **312** | **298** |

Source: *British Rail Motive Power Combined Volume 1980*, Ian Allan Ltd (1979); *British Rail Locomotives 1990*, Ian Allan Ltd (1990)

# Appendix

British Rail main line locomotive fleet on New Year's Eve 1979 and New Year's Eve 1989 (excludes Departmental Locomotives).

## Diesel Locomotives

|  | At 31 December 1979 | At 31 December 1989 |
|---|---|---|
| Class 01 | 1 | 0 |
| Class 03 | 58 | 2 |
| Class 06 | 5 | 0 |
| Class 08 | 879 | 446 |
| Class 09 | 26 | 25 |
| Class 13 | 3 | 0 |
| Class 20 | 217 | 133 |
| Class 24 | 1 | 0 |
| Class 25 | 300 | 0 |
| Class 26 | 42 | 30 |
| Class 27 | 61 | 0 |
| Class 31 | 249 | 186 |
| Class 33 | 94 | 54 |
| Class 37 | 308 | 305 |
| Class 40 | 184 | 0 |
| Class 43 (HST) | 151 | 195 |
| Class 44 | 3 | 0 |
| Class 45 | 126 | 0 |
| Class 46 | 53 | 0 |
| Class 47 | 542 | 406 |